Bibliographic information published by the German National Library:

The German National Library lists this publication in the National Bibliography; detailed bibliographic data are available on the Internet at http://dnb.dnb.de .

Imprint:

Copyright © 2012 GRIN Verlag, Open Publishing GmbH
Print and binding: Books on Demand GmbH, Norderstedt Germany
ISBN: 9783668531550

This book at GRIN:

http://www.grin.com/en/e-book/376247/mobility-supporting-schemes-over-ipv6-networks

Riaz Khan

Mobility Supporting Schemes over IPv6 Networks

GRIN Publishing

GRIN - Your knowledge has value

Since its foundation in 1998, GRIN has specialized in publishing academic texts by students, college teachers and other academics as e-book and printed book. The website www.grin.com is an ideal platform for presenting term papers, final papers, scientific essays, dissertations and specialist books.

Visit us on the internet:

http://www.grin.com/

http://www.facebook.com/grincom

http://www.twitter.com/grin_com

Mobility Supporting Schemes over IPv6 Networks

M.Tech Thesis

Submitted By

Riaz Ahmed Khan

Department of Electronics and Communication Engineering
National Institute of Technology, Srinagar, J&K, India
June 2012

Acknowledgement

*With exception, I would like to express my sincere gratitude to the Almighty **Allah** who is full of mercy and compassion for giving me strength and good health during the whole period of my study.*

I am highly indebted to my mother for her love, blessings, support and encouragement during the days of research.

Finally I thank my friends and not forgetting my course mates for their frankness and availability to discuss diverse social and academic issues, some of whom contributed to this study by providing constructive criticism and moral support.

Abstract

Mobile Internet Protocol (MIP), the current International Engineering Task Force (IETF) proposal for IP mobility support, represents a key element for future all-Internet Protocol (IP) wireless networks to provide service continuity while on the move within a multi-access environment. A performance evaluation of Mobile internet protocol version 6 (IPv6) and its proposed enhancements, i.e., Fast Handovers for Mobile IPv6, Hierarchical Mobile IPv6 was conducted. And a combination of fast handover (FMIPv6) and hierarchical mobile IPv6 (HMIPv6) was proposed and simulated by using the network simulator NS-2. The simulation scenario comprised two access routers and one mobile node that communicated in accordance with the IEEE 802.11 wireless LAN standards. The study provides quantitative results of the performance improvements obtained by the proposed enhancements as observed by a single mobile user with respect to handoff latency, throughput, packet delivery ratio, average jitter etc. In addition to this, the signaling load costs associated with the performance improvements provided by the enhancements has been analyzed. The handover delay reduction approaches, specifically the Fast Handover Mobile Ipv6 FHMIPv6 have been shown. The thesis concludes with the analysis of simulation results, evaluating the MIPv6, HMIPv6 and FHMIPv6 performance and finally gives some suggestions for the future work.

Table of Contents

List of Figures

List of Tables

Acronyms

ARP	Address Resolution Protocol
BS	Base Station
CoA	Care-of-Address
CN	Correspondent Node
DHCP	Dynamic Host Configuration Protocol
DSR	Dynamic Source Routing
DSDV	Destination Sequence Distance Vector
FA	Foreign Agent
FBACK	Fast Binding Acknowledge
FBU	Fast Binding Update
FMIP	Fast Mobile IP
FNA	Fast Neighbor Advertisement
FNAACK	Fast Neighbor Advertisement Acknowledgment
HA	Home Agent
HACK	Handover Acknowledge
HI	Handover Initiate
HMIP	Hierarchical Mobile IP
IETF	Internet Engineering Task Force
LCOA	On-Link Care-of-Address
L2	Layer 2
L3	Layer 3
MAP	Mobility Anchor Point
MN	Mobile Node
NAR	New Access Router
NOAH	NO Ad-Hoc Routing Agent
nFA	New Foreign Agent
oFA	Old Foreign Agent
PAR	Previous Access Router
PrRtAdv	Proxy Router Advertisement
RtSolPr	Router Solicitation for Proxy Advertisement
SCTP	Stream Control Transmission Protocol
SIP	Session Initiation Protocol
WLAN	Wireless Local-area Access Network
WPAN	Wireless Personal-area Access Network

CHAPTER 1: INTRODUCTION

1.1   Research Motivation

The mobile communication is growing very fast in order to meet today world's needs and desires. People are moving from one place to another rapidly, changing their attachment points to the communication networks (Mobile Cellular Networks, Wireless Local Area networks WLAN and Wireless Personal Access Networks WPAN). The main challenge produced by this scenario is how to keep those people connected to their destinations, with the minimum delay, while they are moving among these different wireless and mobile networks.

The fourth generation (4G) of mobile communication networks will be more flexible for users to communicate anywhere anytime. Using the FHMIP and S_MIP connection ability, can facilitate the access to a large number of networks. 4G represents wireless networks integrated with all existing mobile technologies through a common IP core. It consists of an IP based heterogeneous networks, connected together through an IP core using the Internet. Users will be free to move among these networks, and remain connected to their home networks. IP based networks and mobility management are the main features of the 4G communications. Supporting mobility in IP networks will give the possibility to manage the movement between the various wireless networks connected through the Internet.

The high demand for the real time applications through the Internet is one of the challenges in 4G. Real time applications are increasing over the Internet; more and more users are attracted by these kinds of applications, which can be in the form of audio applications, video applications, conference applications and the interactive games. Voice over IP (VoIP) and voice chatting services are the major real time applications used in the Internet. Video streaming, radio and TV over the Internet also are spreading very fast. All these real time applications require a high speed connection with a minimum amount of delay.

Reducing the connection delay and increasing the throughput to satisfy the real time application's requirements must be considered carefully. The goals of supporting mobility

1

around different wireless and mobile networks (the 4G networks), in addition to reduce the connection delay as less as possible in order to satisfy the real time application's requirements, are the main focus in this research. We will concentrate mainly in how to reduce the handover delay to increase the throughput, specifically the mobile IP (MIP) handover delay using a FHMIP approach. Also our focus in this research is on other performance parameters like packet delivery ratio (PDF), packet loss, jitter and end-to-end delay.

1.2   Local and Global Mobility

When IP Mobility is defined within an access network, it becomes a Local Mobility Management Problem. An access network is a collection of fixed and mobile network components belonging to one operational domain and providing access to the internet. The area within which the MN may roam may be restricted, but the overall geographic area might be quite large [1]. The access network gateways act as the aggregation routers. There is administrative management of all the components of the domain defined as local and an association between the components as opposed to none in case of a global mobility management scenario. In case of global mobility management, there is no administrative management between the components and as such there is no restriction of mobility to be within an access network. A comparison of local and global mobility scenario is shown in figure-1.1.

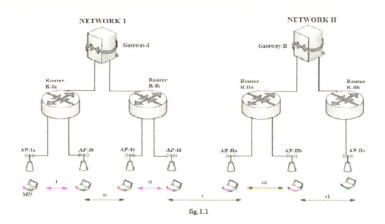

fig.1.1

2

If we have two such networks, Network-I (N-I) and Network-II (N-II), a MN moving between these two access networks will fall into the global mobility scenario and such mobility will be managed by a global mobility protocol like MIPv6, HIP, MOBIKE etc (scenario V in Fig.1.1) . However if a MN moves between two routers of the same access network it will fall in the domain of local mobility and will be managed by a local mobility protocol like PMIPv6 (scenario IV, VI of Fig.1.1). A router having more than one access point implies that any MN movement between the two access points consists of intra-link mobility (scenario I, II, III of Fig.1.1). It involves only Layer 2 mechanisms and as such it is also known as Layer 2 mobility. There is no IP subnet configuration necessary once the MN moves between access points of the same router as the link does not change. However some IP signaling may be required [1]. In case of global mobility protocols, the MN is reachable even when its globally routable IP address changes. Since the basic mobility scenario is the same if the MN moves between routers of the same access network or between routers of different access networks, global mobility protocols can substitute for local mobility protocols. However it is not efficient to use global mobility management protocols for local mobility management. Firstly because updating the CoA at the HA, CN or the global mobility anchor point can be time consuming and results in packet loss when packets continue to be sent to the original or the home address of the MN. Secondly update messages involve signaling between the MN and the HA, or MN and the CN, keeping the MN occupied for some time. This creates performance overhead for the MN as well as the wireless network. Location privacy is another issue with global mobility protocol [1][2][3]. If the CoA of the MN keeps changing, signals need to be exchanged to update the CN, HA or the global mobility anchor point. Traffic analysis can indicate that a particular node in the network is roaming and can also reveal the location of MN. Thus using global mobility management protocols for localized mobility or intra-link mobility has some drawbacks. Therefore need of a localized mobility management protocol arose and gave way to Network - based Localized Mobility Management (NETLMM) [2].

1.3 Host Based Mobility

When the MN is constantly engaged in the process of signaling and such a mobility management approach is known as Host-based mobility management. As there is a Binding Update delay during mobility. If Route Optimization is used, then there might be a further delay before communication might actually start between the MN and the CN. All the messages exchanged by the MN with other agents in the network and with the CN consume bandwidth and cause link layer and IP layer delays. Reducing such delays in the process of handover is essential to the performance improvement of MIPv6. This led to the creation of extended versions of MIPv6, namely HMIPv6 by H.Soliman and FMIPv6 by R.Koodli. A combination of these two led to the creation of FHMIPv6 by HeeYoung Jung et.al.

1.4 Mobile IPv6

Mobile IP supports mobility of IP hosts by allowing them to make use of (at least) two IP addresses: a home address that represents the fixed address of the node and a care-of address (CoA) that changes with the IP subnet the mobile node is currently attached to. Clearly, an entity is needed that maps a home address to the corresponding currently valid CoA. In Mobile IPv4 [4] these mappings are exclusively handled by 'home agents' (HA). A correspondent node (CN) that wants to send packets to a mobile node (MN) will send the packets to the MN's home address. In the MN's home network these packets will be 'intercepted' by the home agent and tunneled, e.g. by IP-in-IP encapsulation [4], either directly to the MN or to a foreign agent to which the MN has a direct link.

In MIPv6, home agents no longer exclusively deal with the address mapping, but each CN can have its own 'binding cache' where home address plus care-of address pairs are stored. This enables 'route optimization' compared to the triangle routing via the HA in MIPv4: a CN is able to send packets directly to a MN when the CN has a recent entry for the MN in its corresponding binding cache. When a CN sends a packet directly to a MN, it does not encapsulate the packet as the HA does when receiving a packet from the CN to be forwarded, but makes use of the IPv6 Routing Header Option. When the CN does not have a binding cache entry for the MN, it sends the packet to the MN's home address. The MN's home agent will then forward the packet. The MN, when receiving an encapsulated packet, will inform the corresponding CN about the current CoA. In order to keep the home address to CoA mappings up-to-date, a mobile node has to signal corresponding changes to its home agent and/or correspondent nodes when performing a handoff to another IP subnet. Since in MIPv6 both HA and CN, maintain binding caches, a common message format called 'binding updates' is used to inform HA and CNs about changes in the point of attachment. Additionally, since the BUs have associated a certain lifetime, even if the MN does not change its location, a BU to its HA and CNs is necessary before the lifetime expires to keep alive the entry in the binding caches. Those Bus are referred as periodic BUs. Binding updates (BU) can be acknowledged by BU Ack (BAck). In contrast to MIPv4, where signaling is done using UDP, Mobile IPv6 signaling is done in extension headers that can also be piggybacked on 'regular' packets. To acquire a CoA in Mobile IPv6, a mobile node can build on IPv6 stateless and stateful auto-configuration methods. The stateless auto configuration mechanism is not available in IPv4. In our work, we assume stateless auto-configuration for all tests since with this mechanism it is not necessary to contact any entity to obtain a new CoA, reducing the handoff process duration. For more details on Mobile IPv6 see [5]. In the following, we briefly look at the Neighbor Discovery [6] mechanism, one of the main differences when comparing IPv4 and IPv6.

1.5   Hierarchical Structures and Protocols

Hierarchical schemes separate mobility management into micro mobility (intra-domain) and macro mobility (inter-domain). They introduce a Mobility Routing Point (MRP) [7] that separates micro from macro mobility. The MRP entity is normally placed at edges of a network, above a set of access/edge routers which constitute the MRP's network domain. The MRP intercepts all packets on behalf of the mobile node (MN) it serves and redirects them to the MN. This enables MNs, which move between access networks that are within the same MRP network domain, to register with the MRP, thus avoiding potential lengthy round-trip delay associated with registration to its home agent. This type of intra-domain mobility is managed by IP Micro mobility management protocols, such as [8] and [9], while inter-domain or macro mobility is almost exclusively managed using Mobile IP.

1.6   Hierarchical Mobile IPv6

It is a well-known observation that MNs moving quickly as well as far away from their respective home domain or correspondent nodes produce significant BU signaling traffic and will suffer from handoff latency and packet losses when no extension to the baseline Mobile IP

5

protocol is used. Hierarchical Mobile IPv6 (HMIPv6) is a localized mobility management proposal that aims to reduce the signaling load due to user mobility. The mobility management inside the local domain is handled by a Mobility Anchor Point (MAP). Mobility between separate MAP domains is handled by MIPv6. The MAP basically acts as a local Home Agent. When a mobile node enters into a new MAP domain it registers with its new MAP, obtaining a regional care-of address (RCoA). The RCoA is the address that the mobile node will use to inform its Home Agent and correspondent nodes about its current location. Then, the packets will be sent to RCoA and intercepted by the MAP, acting as a proxy, and routed inside the domain to the on-link care-of address (LCoA). When a mobile node performs a handoff between two access points within the same MAP domain, only the MAP has to be informed. Note, however that this does not imply any change to the periodic BUs a MN has to send to HA, CNs and now additionally to the MAP. HMIPv6 presents the following advantages: it includes a mechanism to reduce the signaling load in case of handoffs within the same domain and may improve handoff performance reducing handoff latency and packet losses since intra-domain handoffs are performed locally. However, since the periodic BUs are not reduced but the ones due to handoffs, the gain depends on the mobility of the mobile nodes. For more details on HMIPv6 the reader is referred to [10][7].

1.7 FHMIPv6

During the process of handover, there is a time period during which the MN is unable to send or receive any packets. FHMIPv6 is the combination of FMIPv6 and HMIPv6 which was designed to add up the advantages of both and provide additional improvements. It is based on the idea that the MN is aware of the IPv6 subnet it is going to move to before the actual movement takes place. The access router in the foreign network can buffer all the packets destined for the MN that arrive till it actually gets connected after handover.

A MN in its home network has address PCoA (Previous CoA) and is connected to the access router known as the Previous Access Router (PAR). When it moves to the new network, it connects with the New Access Router (NAR) and acquires the New CoA (NCoA). Fast handover consists of three steps: Handover initiation, tunnel establishment and packet forwarding [10][11][12]. FMIPv6 uses Router Solicitation for Proxy Advertisement (RtSolPr) and Proxy

6

Router Advertisement (PrRtAdv) for fast handover. A MN is in its home network can ask its access router for the subnet information of all the access routers that it can detect. Handover is initiated when a MN sends an RtSolPr message to the PAR to indicate that it wants to perform a fast handover to a NAR. This message consists of the link layer address of the new point of attachment that is discovered from the NAR's beacon message. The PAR replies with a PrRtAdv that provides the MN information about the neighboring links and both of these messages together help in expedited movement detection. A tuple (AP-ID, AR-Info) contains an access router's (AR) L2 and IP addresses, and the prefix valid on the interface to which the Access Point (identified by AP-ID) is attached. The triplet (Router's L2 address, Router's IP address, Prefix) is the AR-Info field. This is the tuple that the MN receives when it moves to a new access point with AP-ID. MN finds out the rest of the information from the AR-Info field of the tuple, thus helping in expedited movement detection. MN also forms an NCoA while it is still connected to PAR. Thus this address can be used immediately once movement is detected and address configuration delay is reduced. MN sends a Fast Binding Update (FBU) to the PAR using this NCoA and receives a Fast Binding Acknowledgement (FB-ACK) to indicate success. If it is feasible for MN to send the FBU from the PAR's link, then that should be preferred. Otherwise it should be sent immediately after the NAR has been detected. [21]. A tunnel between the PCoA and the NCoA is created when a PAR sends a Handover Initiation (HI) message to NAR and it replies with a Handover Acknowledgement (Hack). After the tunneling phase is over, packet forwarding starts. PAR begins tunneling packets arriving for PCoA to NCoA. The tunnel remains active until the MN completes the Binding Update with its correspondents. Forwarding support for PCoA is provided through a reverse tunnel between the MN and the PAR since CN's have to be updated with a Binding Cache entry that has the NCoA. MN sends a Fast Neighbor Advertisement (F-NA), to start the packet flow from NAR to itself [12]. Handover can be improvised or optimized using two modes of FMIPv6, Predictive Handover and Reactive Handover. Reactive handover mode is used when a node suddenly loses its connection with its current router or access point. Once the MN is in NAR's link, a FBU is sent and is usually encapsulated in the FNA. The NAR forwards the FBU to the PAR and the PAR starts the tunneling phase after receiving the FBU [11]. FMIPv6 also allows the AR to send an unsolicited PrRtAdv to the MN including the tuple for any neighboring access networks. This is a network initiated handover and may be used for purposes of load sharing [11] .Since

7

FMIPv6 takes care of many things while still in the home network, its handover is faster than a MIPv6 managed mobility network.

1.8   Research Objectives

The main objective of this research is to study the mobility management schemes for next generation, reducing the mobile IP handover delay, study of different performance parameters (packet delivery ratio, packet loss, Average throughput, Average end-to-end delay and Average jitter) in the mobility supporting schemes.

> ➢ Study of Mobile IP approaches (MIPv6, HMIPv6 and FHMIPv6)
> ➢ Simulate Mobile IPv6, Hierarchical Mobile IPv6 and FHMIPv6 protocols using Network Simulator (NS2).
> ➢ The simulation will study the following performance metrics (packet delivery ratio, packet loss, Average throughput, Average end-to-end delay and Average jitter).
> ➢ Compare the simulation results of MIPv6, HMIPV6 and FHMIPv6 approaches.
> ➢ Evaluate the FHMIPv6: in terms of handover delay, packet loss, throughput and network performance as well, compared to MIPv6 and HMIPv6.

1.9   Thesis Outlines

The remaining part of this report is organized as follows: chapter 2 will discuss the mobile IP protocol, IPv4, IPv6, MIPv4 and MIPv6 overview. Then a description for the WLAN as practical example for the MIP will follow. Chapter 3 will cover the literature survey, the mobility support in the present age and problem statement. Chapter 4 will go deeper in the handover delay, reasons and solutions, MIPv6, HMIPv6, FMIPv6 and FHMIPv6 delay equations. Chapter 5 presents the simulation, the simulation model, the simulator and the studied performance metrics. Chapter 6 covers the simulation results, and results analysis. Chapter 7 summarizes the results, concludes the thesis and suggests the future work.

CHAPTER 2: MOBILE IP PROTOCOL (MIP)

2.1 Internet Protocol (IP) Overview

The Internet protocol (IP) provides an unreliable, connectionless delivery mechanism. It defines the basic unit of data transfer through the TCP/IP Internet. Also, IP performs the routing function, choosing a path for data transmission. IP includes the rules for the unreliable data delivery: how hosts and routers process packets, how and when error messages should be generated, and under which conditions packets can be discarded.

IP is responsible from internetwork; interconnects multiple networks (sub networks) into the internet. Getting the packets from the source and deliver them to the destination, this require the pre knowledge about the network topology, the choice of the suitable path, and the avoidance of congestion, this can be done using IP addressing scheme. IPv4 addresses are 32 bits long, and IPv6 addresses are 128 bits long, some part is reserved for the current IPv4 addresses, and the other part is reserved for the link local addresses, which are not routable and unique on the link. These help nodes on the same link in one local network to communicate using their link local addresses without the needs for routers. Nodes know each other, the local routers and the network prefix using neighbor discovery protocol, which will be used by the MIP protocol as well, as will be shown in next section. The IPv6 neighbor discovery protocol is a much improved version of two IPv4 protocols, the address resolution protocol (ARP) and the ICMP router discovery protocol [5].

The main features of IPv6 are:

> ➤ The Hierarchical addresses, to reduce the routing table size in the memory.

> ➤ The simple header, for more fast forwarding and routing process.

> ➤ Security improvement, including the availability of authentication and encryption.

> ➤ The dynamic assignment of addresses.

2.2 IPv4 Addressing and Sub-netting

2.2.1 Hardware Addressing

The hardware address is used by devices to communicate on the local network. Hardware addressing is a function of the data-link layer of the OSI model (Layer-2). The hardware address for Ethernet networks is the MAC address, a 48-bit hexadecimal address that is usually hard-coded on the network card. In theory, this means the MAC address cannot be altered; however, the MAC address is often stored in flash on the NIC, and thus can be changed with special utilities.

MAC addresses can be represented in two formats (either notation is acceptable):

- 00:43:AB:F2:32:13
- 0043.ABF2.3213

The MAC address has one shortcoming – it contains no hierarchy. There is no mechanism to create boundaries between networks [13].

2.2.2 Logical Addressing

- Logical addressing is a function of the network layer of the OSI Model (Layer-3).
- Logical addresses, unlike hardware addresses, provide a hierarchical structure to separate networks. A logical address identifies not only a unique Host ID, but also the network that host belongs to.
- Two common logical addressing protocols are IPX (Internetwork Packet Exchange) and IP (Internet Protocol).

2.3 Internet Protocol (IP)

IP was developed by the Department of Defense (DoD) during the late 1970's. It was included in a group of protocols that became known as the TCP/IP protocol suite.

IP provides two core functions:

- Logical addressing of hosts
- Routing of packets between networks.

IP has undergone several revisions. IP Version 4 (IPv4) was in widespread deployment, but it is going to be replaced with IP Version 6 (IPv6).

2.3.1 IPv4 Addressing

Internet protocol version 4 has been introduced in 1981. IPv4 has performed extremely well in data communication. It provides communication between hosts in a network. The shortcomings of IPv4 is that, it has it has the limited address space, once you fall out of addresses, you won't be able to add any more nodes to the existing network. IPv4 supports 32 bit addressing and each octet is 8 bits long, so there are 4 octets in an IP address [13].

IPv4 header format is shown in the figure-2.1 below:

Vers.=4	IHL	Type of service	Total length	
Identification			Flags	Fragment offset
TTL		Protocol	Header Checksum	
Source Address				
Destination Address				
Options…				

Figure 2.1 IPv4 header

IPv4 has the following problems:

- As the internet is growing at a rapid rate, the IPv4 address space is not scalable.
- Configuration problem, IPv4 needs to be configured manually or by using statefull address configuration protocol (DHCP).
- IPv4 requires security at IP level. There is one standard IPsec but that is optional.

2.3.2   Internet Protocol Version 6 (IPv6)

As the internet is growing and expanding at a rapid rate. The IPv4 is not able to handle the fast demand of IP addresses; therefore there is a need of protocol which can provide large address space, so the new protocol was designed which would never run out of IP addresses, known as internet protocol version 6 or IPv6. IPv6 header format is shown in the figure-2.3 below:

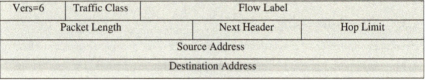

Vers=6	Traffic Class	Flow Label	
Packet Length		Next Header	Hop Limit
Source Address			
Destination Address			

Figure 2.2 IPv6 header

IPv6 has introduced the concept of extension headers [14]. These extension headers can be supplied in order to provide extra information, but encoded in an efficient way. IPv6 has the following extension headers:

- Hop by Hop options: datagrams using this header are called jumbo grams.
- Destination options: holds additional information for the destination.
- Routing: loose list of routers to visit.
- Fragmentation: management of datagrams fragments.
- Authentication: verification of sender's identity.
- Encrypted security payload: information about the encrypted contents.

The features of IPv6 include:

- It will provide addresses to billions of hosts.
- New header format.
- Makes efficient use of router's memory by reducing routing tables and hence faster packet processing capability.
- Improves security of data transfer (authentication and confidentiality). The support for IPsec is mandatory in IPv6.
- Enhances multicasting: reserved multicast addresses which start with "ff".

12

- Auto addressing capability.
- Allows the coexistence of old and new protocols.
- IPv6 has efficient built-in mobility mechanism.
- Better quality of service.

2.4   Mobile IP Version 4 (MIPv4)

The IETF designed a solution for Internet mobility officially called "IP mobility support" and popularly named mobile IP (MIP). The general characteristics include: transparency to application and transport layer protocols, interoperability with IPv4 (using the same addressing scheme), scalability and security.

The mobility challenge is how the host will keep its address while it's moving, without requiring routers to learn host-specific routes. Mobile IP solves this problem by allowing the mobile node to hold two addresses simultaneously. The first is permanent and fixed; it is used by the applications and transport protocols. The second is temporary; it changes as the mobile node moves, and is valid only while the mobile node visits a given location. The mobile node gets the fixed (permanent) address on its original home network. Then it moves to a foreign network and gets the temporary address, after that mobile node must send the temporary address to an agent (router) at home network. The agent then will intercept packets sent to the mobile node's permanent address, and uses encapsulation to tunnel the packets to the mobile node's temporary address. When the mobile node moves again, it gets a new temporary address, and informs the home agent of its new location. When the mobile node back home, it must contact the home agent to stop intercepting the packets. The mobile's fixed address is called the home address, because it is assigned by the home network, and it is a same address like that one assigned to a stationary node. When the mobile node connects to a foreign network, it must obtain the temporary address which is known as a care of address (CoA), with contact to a router in the foreign network called the foreign agent; the mobile node must first discover the foreign agent, and then contact the agent to obtain the care of address. The care of address is treated like any other address on the foreign network [4].

13

Finding the foreign agent (foreign agent discovery mechanism) is done by means of the ICMP router discovery procedure. Routers send an ICMP router advertisement message periodically for each other, and a host sending an ICMP router solicitation to prompt for an advertisement, this process is called the Router discovery mechanism. The foreign agent discovery mechanism added more information to the router discovery message called mobility agent extension. This will allow the foreign agent to advertise its existence and the mobile node to solicit the advertisement [4].

After the mobile node registers with an agent on the foreign network, it must also register with its home agent requesting to forward packets to it care of address. The mobile node sends registration requests to the foreign agent, which forwards it to the home agent.

A Mobile node communicates with other nodes using the following procedure: when the MN sends information to another node, the packets follow the shortest path from the foreign network to the specific destination. The reply will not follow the same route, packets are sent to the mobile's home network first to the home agent, which has registered the mobile's CoA. Second the HA intercepts the packets to distinguish its destination address, and then it encapsulates and tunnels the packets to the care of address. This care of address on the outer datagram specifies the foreign agent, which receives the packets from the home agent, decapsulate them, and then checks its registered mobiles table, and finally transmits the packets to the correct mobile node.

When the mobile node moves to a foreign network and wants to communicate with another node near to the foreign network this causes a delay problem called the triangular routing. Each packet sent to the mobile node travel across the internet to the mobile's home agent which then forwards the packets back again at the foreign network. The problem can be solved using a host specific route, which can be propagating to the nodes near the FAs; this can help eliminating the delay.

14

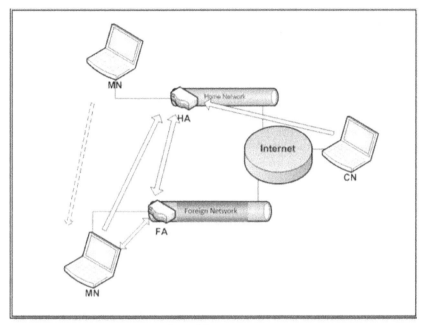

figure-2.3

2.5 Mobile IP Version 6 (MIPv6)

MIPv6 is the modified version of MIPv4, in order to match IPv6 requirements. It has the same protocol architecture as MIPv4, with some differences in the foreign agent discovery process, care of address registration, security and encapsulation enhancement.

Three IPv6 addresses will be assigned to the mobile node: the permanent home address, the current link local address and the care of address, which is associated with the mobile node's home address, only when it is visiting a foreign network. The network prefix of the care of address will be similar to the foreign network prefix, and therefore all packets destined to this care of address will be directly forwarded to the mobile node.

While the mobile node moves from one network to another, the care of address must be configured using stateless address auto configuration or statefull address auto configuration (DHCP) according to the IPv6 neighbor discovery protocol. Mobile node's home address is

15

associated with its CoA, which is known as a binding, MIPv6 is using a binding cache as a central data structure collected by each IPv6 node. After the mobile node has registered its care of address with a home agent, the home agent uses proxy neighbor discovery to intercept IPv6 packets destined to the mobile node's home address, and tunnel them to the mobile node's care of address using IPv6 encapsulation [5].

MIPv6 gives the opportunity to other nodes to communicate directly with the mobile node; a correspondent node will learn the mobile node's binding, adds this binding to the binding cache, and when it sends packets to the mobile node, it forwards them to the mobile node's care of address indicated in the binding cache (this is similar to the existing MIPv4 route optimization).

In order to communicate with the mobile node in the future, the MN registers its CoA with it's HA, and informs correspondent nodes (CNs) with its binding to create or update their binding cache, which is known as the binding update. A binding acknowledgement is sent by a node acknowledging that it receives the binding update. The binding acknowledgement is sent directly to the mobile node, the destination address of the packets carrying the acknowledgement must be the mobile node's care of address which can be known from the binding update message. After receiving the binding update and registering it to the binding cache, the correspondent node (CN) can directly sends packets to the mobile node without the need for forwarding the packets first to the mobile node's home agent. This procedure will help to eliminate the triangular routing problem, which generates longer delay to the packets delivery process [5].

A Mobile node must be able to execute IPv6 decapsulation, send binding updates and receive binding acknowledgment. The same rules apply to the correspondent nodes [5]. In the home network, the mobile node finds out new routers using router discovery protocol based on received routers advertisements messages. The IPv6 neighbor discovery protocol is used by MIPv6 for movement detection as mentioned before. Away from home, mobile node selects one router from the default routers list to be used as a default router, and when the router become unreachable, mobile node must switch to another default router [15].

In the wireless communication case, the mobile node is usually connected to the internet through multiple points of attachments or multiple access routers (wireless coverage overlap). The mobile node will accept packets at its old care of address even after the setup of its new care of address and reports it to the home agent; this makes the handover process smoother among the access routers [16].

MIPv6 is more supporting for security, using IPv6 some security specifications should be considered; authentication required to be implemented by all IPv6 nodes, so the mobile node will be able to send authenticated binding updates [17].

MIPv6 adds more overhead than MIPv4, because the sending of a binding update not just to the home agent but also to all the correspondent nodes (CN) that the MN will connect to them. There is also extra overhead produced from the binding acknowledgement exchange. All this extra overhead will affect the handover delay for the mobile node while it is moving, and probably increasing the handover delay.

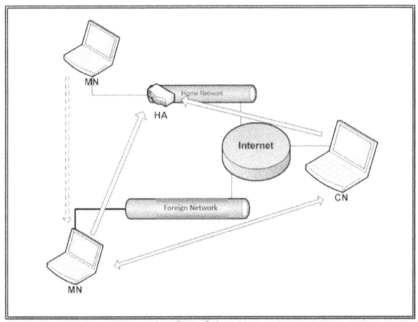

figure-2.4

2.6 Wireless Local Area Networks (WLAN)

WLAN is spreading very fast, because it has the ability to support mobility using wireless coverage and MIP protocol, its flexibility and its fast installation. WLAN products use the free industrial, scientific, and medical (ISM band, 2.4 GHz), which makes the owners, operators and users do not need permission for deploying the service and using it.

IEEE 802.11 is the most famous WLAN standard; it takes in specifications for medium access and radio transmission technology for ISM based WLAN: the MAC layer protocol, the physical layer protocol and also it offers same interface to upper layer protocols as regular 802.x LANs (Ethernet) [18].

Wireless LAN offers high data rates, it reaches up to 54Mbps (the highest data rate provided by a wireless network for indoor applications). Wireless LAN supports a layer 2 handover when the mobile node switches from one access point to another. MIP is used among the IP core connected WLAN access points to perform the handover process. MIP is working independently for link layer (L2) technologies which cost more overhead to perform the handover; in the WLAN when the mobile node moves from one access router to another it first perform a link layer handover (according to the signal strength procedure), then the MIP handover will take place, which will require another time to be setup and to continue the ongoing communication [17].

In WLAN L2 handover is used to change access routers, which cause interruption for the transmitted data (L2 handover delay). Layer 2 handover is needed in the following: movement detection, searching for new access router and reconnection. The mobile node, the old access router and the new access router are the participating nodes in the handover process. Then the L3 MIP handover will start because the mobile node can just communicate with the foreign agent with the same link. MIP handover involves two processes: agent discovery and agent registration as mentioned before [24] [19].

CHAPTER 3: LITERATURE SURVEY

With the development of network technology, Ipv6 will be widely used in the next generation Internet, IPv6 could combine mobile networks and fixed wireless networks closely, which brings great convenience to people's live. The handoff delay of Mobile IPv6 seriously affected the real-time communication service quality, therefore various improvement methods based on the basic Mobile IPv6 protocol are proposed.

With the fast development of wireless technology and high-performance mobile devices such as mobile phones, Pocket PC, portable computers and so on, users hope to connect the internet at anytime, anywhere. In order to meet the needs of the people on the mobile Internet; we need to study the Mobile IP technology.

In November 1996, IETF announced a draft agreement on Mobile IPv6 [20]. After 24 versions of the improvement, it was submitted as the standard Mobile IPv6 protocol, which still has more problems to be solved, such as security, handoff delay, multicast and so on. In order to achieve seamless roaming, switching performance, the basic Mobile IPv6 protocol switch method had to be improved. So various methods and approaches were proposed by different research scholars and scientists. The approaches and methods that I studied during my literature survey for Mobile IP and are as follows:

Zongpu Jia, Gaolei Wang and Ran Zhao in their paper "A Literature Survey on Handoff for Mobile IPv6" gave a brief survey on handoff for MIPv6. They stated that with the development of network technology, IPv6 will be widely used in the next generation Internet, IPv6 could combine mobile networks and fixed wireless networks closely, which brings great convenience to people's live. The handoff delay of Mobile IPv6 seriously affected the real-time communication service quality, therefore various improvement methods based on the basic Mobile IPv6 protocol are proposed. They described the working principle of Mobile IPv6, the current main switch methods were summarized and the typical methods were detailed and compared in their paper [20][21].

19

Xavier P´erez-Costa, Marc Torrent-Moreno and Hannes Hartenstein in their paper titled as "A Performance Comparison of Mobile IPv6 and its extensions" conducted a performance evaluation of Mobile IPv6 and its proposed enhancements, i.e., Fast Handovers for Mobile IPv6, Hierarchical Mobile IPv6 using the network simulator ns-2. Their study provides quantitative results of the performance improvements obtained by the proposed enhancements as observed by a single mobile user with respect to handoff latency, packet loss rate and achieved bandwidth per station. As a complementary part of the study, the signaling load costs associated with the performance improvements provided by the enhancements has been analyzed [10] [22].

Hesham Soliman, in his paper titled as "Hierarchical MIPv6 mobility management (HMIPv6)"- July 2001 stated as hierarchical mobility management for MIPv6 will reduce the amount of signaling to CNs and the HA and may also improve the performance of MIPv6 in terms of handoff speed. Moreover, HMIPv6 is well suited to implement access control and handoffs between different access technologies [7].

Petri Jokela, Teemu Rinta-aho, et al., in their paper "Handover Performance with HIP and MIPv6" have proposed that One problem with the current Internet architecture is that the IP address is used both for describing the topological location of the host and, at the same time, to identify the host. The Host Identity Protocol (HIP) is one proposal to solve this semantic overloading of IP addresses. Also they compare the handover performance between Mobile IPv6 and HIP based mobility management in a heterogeneous IPv6 network environment. They made mobile host to move between WLAN and GPRS networks, and the mobility management is handled purely on layer 3 without any performance optimization approaches [23].

Chao Fan, lun Liu and Wei Guo in their paper "Implement Scheme of MIPv6 and Improvement of hand over delay based on Adhoc network on Linux" have implemented MIPv6 protocol on Linux. In different network topologies verifying the feasibility and validity of test, they improve the segment affecting handoff delay. By building the scene of testing, the delay is obtained. They concluded that the handoff delay can be reduced by modifying parameters to optimizing protocol. Finally on account of packet loss which brought by single network card, they propose the mechanism of dual NIC which can effectively solve the handoff delay caused by changing working mode of network card [24].

Xinyi WU and Gang NIE in their paper titled "Comparison of Different Mobility Management Schemes for reducing handover Latency in Mobile IPv6" presented a comparative study of some different mobility management scheme for reducing handover latency and packet loss in mobile IPv6 environment. They described the different types and classification of handover and present the Macro-Mobility and the Micro-Mobility solutions, including a number of proposals to reduce handover latency for mobile IPv6. The discussion regarding the performance of each proposed methods and the comparison of the performance between each method are also brought up [25].

Hong-Sun Jun and Miae Woo in their paper "Performance Analysis of Multicast-based Localized Mobility Support Scheme in IPv6 Networks" proposed a multicast-based localized mobility support scheme in order to compensate the drawbacks of Mobile IPv6. The proposed scheme utilizes Mobile IPv6 for the macro mobility and PIM-SM in the visited domain. Performance of the proposed scheme is evaluated by simulation and the results are compared with those of Mobile IPv6. The proposed scheme gives lesser packet loss as compared to MIPv6 and is 91% lesser packet loss was observed [26].

Rajeev Koodli in his paper "IP Address Location Privacy and Mobile IPv6" has discussed Location Privacy as applicable to Mobile IPv6. We document the concerns arising from revealing Home Address to an on-looker and from disclosing Care of Address to a correspondent [27].

Shaima Qureshi , M. Ahsan Chishti and Ajaz H. Mir in their paper "Mobility Management in Next Generation Networks" have overview Local and global mobility with respect to the protocols of the next generation internet. MIPv6 leading all of them has been improvised by its extensions namely HMIPv6, FMIPv6 etc, all of whom are host based. NETLMM has come up to set up a mobility management network without involving MN in the procedure. This increases

21

the scope of nodes participating in mobility. Signaling involved in handover and the total handover latency in each of the protocols has been compared. They suggested that these protocols can be used in conjunction with latest technologies like Source Specific Multicast (SSM) and can be studied for mobile internet related applications involving audio, video streaming and other real time communications. They again suggested that both mobility and SSM find their application in upcoming fields like e-learning, IP-television etc [28].

Takeshi Takahashi, Koichi Asataniz and Hideyoshi Tominaga in their paper titled "Multicast Source Handover Scheme based on Proxy Router Discovery" proposed that in order To support multicast over Mobile IP networks, the IETF proposed two schemes, namely bi-directional tunneling (MIP-BT) and remote subscription (MIP-RS). MIP-BT provides mobility by establishing bi-directional tunnel from home agent to mobile node's care-of address. Although it does not require multicast tree reconstruction, it suffers from redundant routing that causes packet delivery delay and network bandwidth consumption. On the other hand, MIP-RS provides mobility by reconstructing multicast tree when mobile node enters a foreign network. Although MIP-RS provides shortest multicast routing path, it requires the reconstruction of entire multicast tree in case of source mobility and causes service disruption time during the process of handover.

To cope with those problems, they proposed new source mobility scheme that enjoys the advantages of MIP-RS and provides seamless handover with the help of proxy router, which assists handover by swapping network addresses and conducting packet forwarding. they examined the deployment issues of the proposed scheme over the Internet and evaluate the proposed scheme from the viewpoint of routing distance and network bandwidth consumption through simulation experiments with various parameters, and then clarify the effectiveness and efficiency of the proposed scheme.

David N. Cottingham and Pablo A. Vidales in their paper "Is Latency the Real Enemy in Next Generation Networks?" suggested the idea that apart from the network vertical handover latency effects on the TCP/IP stack, there is another challenge that shadows ubiquitous networking. The TCP-connection adaptation time required when roaming between two disparate wireless technologies can be even longer than the total handover period. Thus, the impact of the adaptation time needs to be minimized and considered when dealing with seamless networking in heterogeneous environments. They presented an experimental test bed that has been used to characterize the latency during vertical handover. Later, they introduced the concept of adaptation time (t_a) and show the experimental value of t_a, obtained from the collected traces. Finally, they discuss the effects of t_a on the TCP/IP stack during heterogeneous handovers [29].

Jianfeng Guan, Yajuan Qin, Shuai Gao, and Hongke Zhang in their paper "The Performance Analysis Of Multicast In Proxy Mobile Ipv6" have studied the PMIPv6 and proposed two PMIPv6 multicast methods called the (Mobile Access Gateway) MAG-based method and (Local Mobility Anchor) LMA-based method to provide the multicast routing. they simulate two multicast methods to evaluate and compare their performance. The simulation results show that the MAG-based method has lower end-to-end delay and larger multicast handover delay, while the LMA-based method has the larger end-to-end delay and lower multicast handover delay [30].

X. M. Xiao and J. Lei proposed an analytical method and compared the PMIPv6 with other mobility support protocols, and the results show that PMIPv6 may cause high handover latency when LMA is far from the current MAG [30].

Zhou et al. Proposed a fast handover scheme based on the FMIPv6 operation and IEEE 802.21 link layer triggers to improve the PMIPv6 and it has lower handover latency than PMIPv6 [30].

K. S. Kong et al. analyzed the handover latency of the PMIPv6 and compared it with MIPv6 and its variants. The analytical results show that the PMIPv6 has the much lower handover latency than MIPv6 [30].

Huei-Wen Ferng, Wen-Yan Kao, Jeng-Ji Huang, and David Shiung in their paper "A Dynamic Resource Reservation Scheme Designed for Improving Multicast Protocols in HMIPv6-Based Networks" aimed at proposing a dynamic resource reservation scheme to enhance wireless multicasting protocols run in the hierarchical mobile IP version 6 (HMIPv6) based networks. The novelty of their scheme relies on techniques of dynamic resource

23

reservation, priority, pre-registration, and path prediction, which are used to improve wireless multicasting and guarantee service continuity. Through numerical examples, they demonstrated that the proposed scheme performs well in terms of robustness, adaptiveness, and quality of service (QoS) guarantee [29].

Yen-Wen Chen, and Ming-Jen Huang in their paper "A Novel MAP Selection Scheme by Using Abstraction Node in Hierarchical MIPv6" focused on the selection of the mobility anchor point (MAP) in hierarchical mobile IPv6 (HMIPv6) environment. An enhanced speed estimation method was provided in their paper to reduce the estimation error. Furthermore, the concept of abstract MAP (AMAP) node is proposed so that the frequency of inter domain handoff can be effectively reduced and the load among MAP nodes can be more balanced in HMIPv6. The performance of the proposed scheme is examined through exhaustive simulations. Their simulation results show that the proposed scheme can achieve the desired objective. The proposed scheme was speed estimation scheme based on the correlation between the latest estimated speed and average speed.

Myung-Kyu Yi, Jin-Woo Choi, and Young-Kyu Yang in their paper titled "A Comparative Analysis on the Signaling Load of Proxy Mobile IPv6 and Hierarchical Mobile IPv6" investigated the performance of the proxy mobile IPv6 and compare it with that of the hierarchical mobile IPv6. It is well known that performance of proxy mobile IPv6 is better than that of hierarchical mobile IPv6. For the more detailed performance analysis, they proposed an analytic mobility model based on the random walk to take into account various mobility conditions. Based on the analytic models, they formulate the location management cost and handoff management cost. Then, they analyze the performance of the proxy mobile IPv6 and hierarchical mobile IPv6, respectively. The numerical results show that the proxy mobile IPv6 can has superior performance to hierarchical mobile IPv6 by reducing the latencies for location update and handoff [31] [32] [8].

Long Le and Marco Liebsch in their paper "Preliminary Binding: An Extension to Proxy Mobile IPv6 for Inter-Technology Handover" investigated technical issues that occur during an inter technology handover in Proxy Mobile IPv6. They demonstrate through experimental performance evaluation that an inter-technology handover in Proxy Mobile IPv6 can cause considerable handover delay and packet loss. They proposed an efficient extension to Proxy Mobile IPv6 to eliminate delay and packet loss during an inter-technology handover. They demonstrate the effectiveness of the proposed extension through an experimental performance evaluation [33].

Wang Lixin, Jian Yingxia, Zheng Dawer and Chen Zhixin in their paper titled "HMIPv6-based Handover Optimized Solution and Performance Analysis" introduced a MIPv6-based handover optimized solution for inter domain handover management to reduce the binding update and packet delivery delay and traffic. In contrast with the normal HMIP protocol, the method can largely reduce the handoff latency and packets loss. Then based on the balance of the wireless link efficiency and the packet loss ratio, how the agent advertisement period affects the handoff performance in their proposal is analyzed. Finally, they obtained the optimal agent advertisement period of our handover optimized solution [8].

3.1   Problem Statement

After doing a thorough study of the Mobile IP approaches, I came into a problem that needs to be addressed in order to provide uninterrupted service to mobile users. That problem is the handover delay reduction. Literature survey reveals that the MIP extensions should be optimized so that the handover delay should be as minimum as possible and also the throughput should be increased or well-maintained so that the mobile users can get uninterrupted service while a handoff occurs. Other performance parameters like packet delivery ratio, end-to-end delay and jitter should also be taken into consideration. So the next chapters will cover all these performance metrics and a simulation study of MIP approaches specifically FHMIPv6 in order to reduce the handover delay.

CHAPTER 4: HANDOVER DELAY

A mobile node (MN) using MIP to support mobility will perform several tasks: exchanging information and signaling with the Home Agent (HA) and the Foreign Agent (FA) after it moves, a mobile node must detect that it has moved, communicate across the foreign network to obtain a secondary address, and then communicate across the internet to its home agent to arrange packet forwarding. It requires considerable overhead after each move.

Handover delay is the time taken for redirecting the ongoing connection, when the mobile node changes its attachment point from one to another (i.e. terminating the existing connection and establishing a new connection). The handover delay is comprised of two distinct delays: First the time taken for the HA registration process, named as registration delay. Second the time taken for MN to configure a new network care of address in the foreign network called address resolution delay; both combined represent the overall handover delay in mobile IP (MIP).

Delay reduction solutions are mainly focus to reduce the HA registration delay and the FA address resolution delay. Hierarchical network structure approach is suggested to minimize the registration delay using hierarchical handover. For the address resolution delay, an address pre-configuration is suggested to minimize the delay time using fast handover approach. A combined hierarchical and fast approach also is suggested to improve the performance of mobile IP [11].

4.1   Handover Delay Reasons

When a node changes its network, it has to identify its movement. The node figures out this movement by matching its IP address prefix with the prefix of the network. This is known as the *movement detection delay* (T_{mdd}). Once the movement is detected, the node has to wait for a router advertisement. A router advertisement is a message that is sent out periodically by a router to a multicast capable link to announce its availability. If the node receives no such advertisement, the node itself sends a router solicitation to get a router advertisement message immediately. These advertisements and solicitations' help in router, prefix and parameter

26

discovery as well as address auto configuration [34]. This introduces another kind of delay known as the *router advertisement delay*. Once the router is recognized and a new IP address obtained in the foreign network, there is an IP address check to ensure that there is no duplication of IP addresses. The time taken is known as the *duplicate address detection delay*. The router advertisement delay and the duplicate address detection delay together represented as T_{dadd} is followed by more delays before communication can be restored. The signals and notifications exchanged between the node and its home network introduces the *binding update delay* (T_{bud}). In certain applications long delays cause packet discarding at the destination [28]. If route optimization is used, then additional time is required to register the new CoA with the CN (T_{ro}). The updates to the HA and the CN are sent through notifications. The CoA is communicated using these notification procedures. The MN can send a Binding Update to a correspondent and later the correspondent can send packets directly to MN, without having HA as an intermediate [34]. This is done using Route Optimization supported in Mobile IPv6. Route Optimization uses Return Routability Procedure [18]. It involves two kinds of checks to ensure that there is a node to which packets can be sent and accepted from. The Home Address check and the CoA check consist of messages that are sent to the HA and the CN respectively.

4.1.1 Standard MIPv6 Handover Delay

In MIPv6 protocol before communication is re-established between MN and CN, signals are exchanged. The total time (T_M) required for the handover is the sum of the delays as described earlier.

$$T_M = T_{mdd} + T_{dadd} + T_{bud}$$

If Route Optimization is used then the total handover time is equal to:

$$T_{MRO} = T_{mdd} + T_{dadd} + T_{bud} + T_{ro}$$

4.1.2 HMIPv6 Handover Delay

In HMIPv6, the introduction of MAP reduces the BU messages exchanged between the HA and the MN. Therefore the handover delay of HMIPv6 consists of the factors T_{mdd}, T_{dadd} and T'_{bud}, where T'_{bud} is the new binding update delay that is smaller than its counterpart in MIPv6. Since MAP is closer to the MN than a HA, HMIPv6 gets the advantage over MIPv6 protocol by having a network entity closer to the MN and also hiding the location of the MN from the CN and HA. Therefore,

$$T_H = T_{mdd} + T_{dadd} + T'_{bud}$$

4.1.3 FMIPv6 Handover Delay

In FMIPv6, the CoA configuration and the duplicate address detection is done before it disconnects from the link to the network it was previously in. Therefore T_{dadd} is removed from T_M. Therefore the total handover latency time (T_F) of FMIPv6 can be expressed as:

$$T_F = T_{mdd} + T_{bud}$$

Fast handover mechanism has an advantage over MIPv6 and HMIPv6 because the term T_{dadd} is missing from the expression for total handover latency.

4.1.4 FHMIPv6 Handover Delay

If we use F-HMIPv6 protocol, then we get rid of the term T_{dadd} from the total time as well as get the reduced T'_{bud} time for binding updates making the total time for a F-HMIPv6 protocol as follows:

$$T_F = T_{mdd} + T'_{bud}$$

The best handover latency is achieved when FMIPv6 and HMIPv6 are used together as is done in F-HMIPv6 protocol. The result is signaling load reduction, improvement in latency delay and less packet losses apart from helping the handover process by pre-configuration of CoA.

28

CHAPTER 5: THE SIMULATION

5.1 Simulation Goals

The simulation process has been done in the following steps: first building the simulation model of the mobile IP network, second implement the mobile IP model in a computer program using (Network Simulator NS2), third run the program and get the performance metrics, finally analyze the results according to the protocol behavior in the network system. In order to evaluate the mobile IP handover delay reduction approaches we will study the network performance using the simulation tool (NS-2). The main goal of the simulation is to study the effects of the FHMIPv6 scheme on the handover delay of an end to end TCP communication session, and then compare it to the handover delay for the standard MIPv6 and HMIPv6.

The network Simulator NS-2.31 allinone package over linux OS was used to simulate the network topology shown in figure 5.1 and figure 5.2. A patch namely "FHMIP-1.3-extension" was used for the studied scenario. There is another patch namely "MOBIWAN" that can be used for the same purpose but we did not use that in our simulation scenario. We only used ns-FHMIP-1.3 extension on NS-2.31 [35, 36].

5.2 Simulation Model

NS2 supports wireless and standard MIP protocol model. The mobile nodes are independent; each one has one or more interfaces to the wireless channel. The main function of the channel is to distribute the packets to all the network interfaces. There are also gateways between the wired and wireless nodes named base station (BS) nodes to facilitate packets routing between wired and wireless networks.

5.3 Mobile IP Extension

First we used the basic mobile IP extension of NS2 to simulate the standard MIP protocol. The NS2 MIP extension consists of a mobile host MH, a home agent HA and a foreign agent FA or foreign agents FAs. The MH is a mobile node, the HA and FA are BS nodes. The HA and FA

29

have registration agent, which sends beacons to the mobile nodes, performs encapsulation and decapsulation, and reply to solicitations from mobile nodes. The MH also have a registration agent, which responds to the beacons and sends solicitations to the HA and FA. When the mobile node moves from one network to another it changes the care of address. All the packets which destined to the mobile node will be tunneled by the HA to the mobile node's CoA.

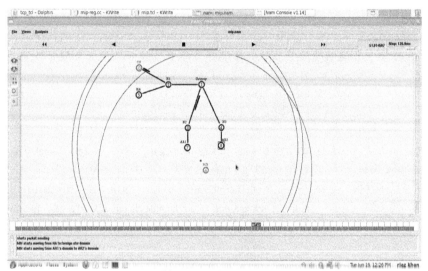

Figure 5.1 MIPv6

The basic MIP extension to NS does not consider other handover protocols like reducing signaling load in the external network and pre-address configuration etc. The thing made us search for another NS extension, which has more consideration to the other MIP handover delay reduction methods.

5.3.1   Delay Reduction Extensions to NS2

In order to simulate the handover delay reduction mechanisms we used the HMIP and FHMIP extension to NS2. The new additions are the MAP agent and the Fast handover functionality. The MAP agent can be connected to a normal wired node which makes it play the MAP role as a gateway between the mobile node' HA and FA. The MAP receives the tunneled packets from the

30

HA and then forwards them after decapsulation encapsulation processes to the access router (AP) under its domain. The HA, PAR and NAR are sending advertisements beacons (advertisement message-ad) every second, when the MN receives the **adv** messages it registers with the sending base station node, then the MN propagates the registration to the HA.

The mobile node's behavior when it reaches the range of the NAR:
Standard MIP: As long as the MN receives advertisements ad messages from the PAR, it ignores the ad messages from the NAR. When the MN loses the connection with the PAR (3 seconds time out) the MN sends a registration request to the NAR and then changes its CoA.

HMIP: The MN registration is updated every second and propagated to the MAP and HA, as long as the MN moves inside the domain of the MAP and no need to reregister with the HA every single time and CN as well.

FMIP: The MN registers itself with the NAR immediately after receiving a new ad message from it. First the MN sends RTSOLPR message to the PAR, which sends handoff initiate (HI) message to the NAR and after getting an acknowledgement (HACK) from NAR, it builds a tunnel. The PAR sends PRRTADV message to the MN, which sends a registration request to the NAR and then the NAR forwards it to the HA.

FHMIP: Here we have a mix between the HMIP and the FMIP functionality, when the MN receives an **ad** message (beacon message) from the NAR, it sends RTSOLPR message to the PAR. The PAR and NAR exchange HI-HACK messages but do not build up a tunnel. The PAR sends PRRTADV message to the MN, which request a registration from the NAR. The NAR forwards the registration request to the MAP which starts forwarding the packets destined to the MN to the NAR. This will reduce the packet losses because the packet forwarding will not be started until the registration is completed.

5.4 Simulation Scenario

Figure 5.2 shows the simulated network topology: a hierarchical address is used for all the nodes. There are five domains: the wired nodes, the correspondent node, the home agent HA, the foreign agent FA (PAR and NAR) and the mobile node (MN). This network topology is the simplest one that we have designed for mobile IP performance evaluation and studies. The two access routers are set close together to ensure a partial overlapping between their coverage areas, also helps in handover delay reduction.

In this simulation we only consider a linear movement pattern for the mobile node, the mobile node will move linearly between the access routers from one to another at varying speeds (1m/s to 10m/s-15m/s -20m/s). Then we calculated the different performance metrics on these varying speeds of MN. The simulation begins when the mobile node MN is inside the HA's domain positioned near to HA and starts a TCP session with CN and receives TCP packets through HA. Then the mobile node starts moving to MAP's domain near to PAR and stops receiving packets through HA and starts receiving packets through PAR. Then again MN shows a movement from PAR to NAR and gets disconnected from PAR and attached to NAR and receives packets through NAR. A TCP source agent is attached to the correspondent node (CN) and a TCP sink agent attached to the mobile node (MN). The TCP source agent is connected to a traffic generator which is the only source for the ongoing traffic among the network.

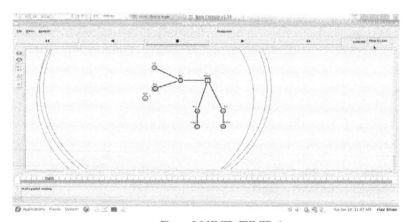

Figure 5.2 HMIP, FHMIPv6

32

CHAPTER 6: THE RESULTS

The simulation results are obtained after simulation of network topologies for MIPv6, HMIPv6 and FHMIPv6. Different trace files were obtained after simulation. These trace files were analyzed by using AWK scripts to obtain results for different performance parameters. We obtained the results for the Mobile IP approaches first by varying the speed of mobile node and secondly by increasing the simulation time. Below are the results for different performance metrics at varying speed of MN and at increasing simulation time.

6.1 Results Obtained By Varying the Speed of MN

Performance Metrics	FHMIPv6	HMIPv6	MIPv6
Gen. or sent packets	11878	10780	10775
Received Pkts.	11458	8342	6709
Pkt. delivery Ratio (%)	96.4641	77.3840	62.2645
Dropped pkts	84	133	147
Avg end-to-end delay(ms)	8.7597	8.73147	8.73142
Control packets	11761	10674	10671
Avg. routing Load	39.2033	35.58	35.57
Avg.throughput (kbps)	610.42	552.66	541.27
Avg. handover-Delay (secs.)	0.05544	2.10225	3.24393
Avg. jitter (secs)	0.00554	0.02923	0.37122

Table 6.1- while MN is moving at speed 1m/s

Performance Metrics	FHMIPv6	HMIPv6	MIPv6
Gen. or sent Packets	11740	10661	10650
Received Pkts.	11316	8251	6634
Pkt. delivery Ratio (%)	96.3884	77.3942	62.2910
Dropped Pkts	98	130	141
Avg end-to-end delay(ms)	8.7596	8.73142	8.73136
Control Packets	11614	10563	10548
Avg. routing Load	38.7133	35.21	35.16
Avg.throughput (kbps)	602.65	546.66	537.67
Avg. handover-Delay (secs.)	0.22552	2.17132	3.26544
Avg. jitter (secs)	0.00549	0.03148	0.37142

Table 6.2- while MN is moving at speed 2m/s

Performance Metrics	FHMIPv6	HMIPv6	MIPv6
Gen. or sent packets	11944	10651	10658
Received Pkts.	11514	8244	6639
Pkt. delivery Ratio (%)	96.3999	77.4011	62.2912
Dropped pkts	94	124	137
Avg end-to-end delay (ms)	8.7597	8.73147	8.73144
Control packets	11818	10572	10578
Avg. routing Load	39.3933	35.17	35.26
Avg.throughput(kbps)	612.59	546.87	538.11
Avg. handover delay (secs)	1.31775	2.38745	3.11875
Avg. jitter (secs)	0.00554	0.03374	0.38471

Table 6.3- while MN is moving at speed 3m/s

Performance Metrics	FHMIPv6	HMIPv6	MIPv6
Gen. or sent packets	11276	10752	10746
Received Pkts.	10867	8290	6673
Pkt. delivery Ratio (%)	96.3728	77.1019	62.0975
Dropped pkts	102	127	142
Avg end-to-end delay (ms)	8.73145	8.73141	8.73137
Control packets	10664	10669	10664
Avg. routing load	37.42	35.27	35.14
Avg.throughput (kbps)	608.24	544.19	527.09
Avg. handover-delay (secs)	1.30927	2.37554	3.11875
Avg. jitter (secs)	0.00577	0.03469	0.39451

Table 6.4- while MN is moving at speed 4m/s

Performance Metrics	FHMIPv6	HMIPv6	MIPv6
Gen. or sent packets	11461	10753	10778
Received Pkts.	11046	8321	6711
Pkt. delivery Ratio (%)	96.3790	77.3840	62.2657
Dropped pkts	99	118	127
Avg. end-to-end delay (ms)	8.7596	8.73145	8.73144
Control packets	11338	10652	10658
Avg. routing load	37.7933	35.47	35.4912
Avg. throughput(kbps)	611.13	549.27	531.91
Avg. handover-delay (secs)	1.89625	2.46546	3.24442
Avg. jitter (secs)	0.00595	0.03621	0.41792

Table 6.5- while MN is moving at speed 5m/s

Performance Metrics	FHMIPv6	HMIPv6	MIPv6
Gen. or sent packets	11514	10340	10748
Received Pkts.	11100	8003	6759
Pkt. delivery Ratio (%)	96.4044	77.3984	62.8861
Dropped pkts	86	109	111
Avg. end-to-end delay (ms)	8.7596	8.73147	8.73146
Control packets	11406	10191	10658
Avg. routing load	38.02	33.97	34.12
Avg. throughput(kbps)	612.02	551.07	536.24
Avg. handover-delay (secs)	2.01175	2.77228	3.27479
Avg. jitter (secs)	0.00576	0.03589	0.40265

Table 6.6- while MN is moving at speed 6m/s

Performance Metrics	FHMIPv6	HMIPv6	MIPv6
Gen. or sent packets	11538	10721	10721
Received Pkts.	11108	8296	6756
Pkt. delivery Ratio (%)	96.2732	77.3808	63.0165
Dropped pkts	104	111	113
Avg. end-to-end delay (ms)	8.7596	8.73145	8.73140
Control packets	11400	10242	10602
Avg. routing Load	38.17	34.22	34.07
Avg. throughput (kbps)	609.11	549.91	534.37
Avg. handover-delay (secs)	2.54317	2.89503	3.36482
Avg. jitter (secs)	0.00569	0.03321	0.37143

Table 6.7- while MN is moving at speed 7m/s

Performance metrics	FHMIPv6	HMIPv6	MIPv6
Gen. or sent packets	11742	10736	10727
Received Pkts.	11324	8309	6803
Pkt. delivery Ratio (%)	96.4401	77.3938	63.4194
Dropped pkts	90	104	107
Avg. end-to-end delay (ms)	8.7596	8.73142	8.73141
Control packets	11624	10655	10634
Avg. routing load	38.7567	35.5167	35.1712
Avg. throughput (kbps)	613.87	554.29	539.67
Avg. handover-delay (secs)	2.89513	2.98445	3.42582
Avg. jitter (secs)	0.00552	0.03299	0.36161

Table 6.8- while MN is moving at speed 8m/s

Performance Metrics	FHMIPv6	HMIPv6	MIPv6
Gen. or sent packets	11502	10708	10691
Received Pkts.	11094	8289	6781
Pkt. delivery Ratio(%)	96.4528	77.4094	63.4271
Dropped pkts	76	96	101
Avg. end-to-end delay (ms)	8.7596	8.73047	8.73046
Control packets	11398	10616	10566
Avg. routing load	37.9933	35.3867	35.0024
Avg. throughput(kbps)	614.72	555.16	541.00
Avg. handover-delay (secs)	2.90425	3.08722	3.56149
Avg. jitter (secs)	0.00564	0.03317	0.38172

Table 6.9- while MN is moving at speed 9m/s

Performance metrics	FHMIPv6	HMIPv6	MIPv6
Gen. or sent packets	11450	10695	10686
Received Pkts.	11038	8276	6775
Pkt. delivery Ratio (%)	96.4017	77.3819	63.4007
Dropped pkts	88	102	107
Avg. end-to-end delay (ms)	8.7596	8.73142	8.73140
Control packets	11338	10580	10585
Avg. routing load	37.7933	35.2667	34.9727
Avg. throughput (kbps)	612.13	552.71	538.76
Avg. handover-delay (secs)	2.39941	2.67243	3.24234
Avg. jitter (secs)	0.00573	0.03419	0.3995

Table 6.10- while MN is moving at speed 10/ms

Similar results were obtained from the simulation when MN was kept at moving speed of 15m/s and 20m/s.

After obtaining the results we plotted them for different performance metrics. The simulation results for standard MIPv6, HMIPv6 and FHMIPv6 models are shown below. The results compare between the "packet delivery ratio, average handover delay, average throughput and average jitter". First we showed the results for varying speed of MN.

- **Packet Delivery Ratio By Varying The Speed Of MN**

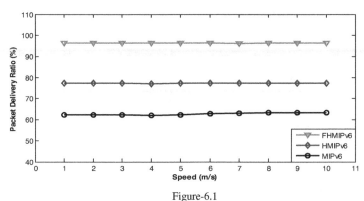

Figure-6.1

- **Average Throughput By Varying The Speed Of MN**

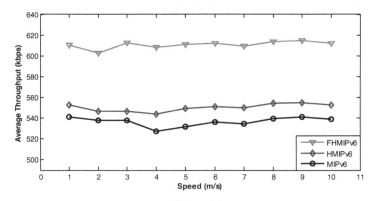

Figure-6.2

36

Figure-6.1 shows the PDF comparison for FHMIPv6, HMIPv6 and MIPv6 approaches. It can be seen from the figure that FHMIPv6 has more packet delivery ratio (received packets/sent packets) as compared to other two approaches. As we varied the speed of MN, we observed that it does not affect the percentage of delivered packets. It remains almost same with very little variations. The maximum PDFs obtained for FHMIP, HMIP and MIP are 96%, 77% and 63% respectively.

Figure-6.2 shows the average throughput comparison among FHMIPv6, HMIPv6 and standard MIPv6. We observed that the throughput in case of FHMIPv6 is more with respect to HMIPv6 and MIPv6 as we have already seen the PDF is more for FHMIPv6 and hence more data is transferred per unit time in FHMIPv6 approach and considered to be efficient one approach. The maximum throughput obtained for FHMIP, HMIP and MIP is 614kbps, 555kbps and 541 respectively.

- **Average Handover Delay By Varying The Speed Of MN**

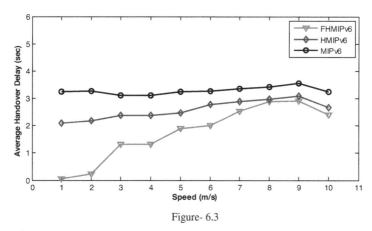

Figure- 6.3

From the figure-6.3, it is observed that the handover delay for FHMIP is lesser than the other two approaches. It follows a trend FHMIP<HMIP<MIP in terms of average handover delay. The reason behind this is the pre-address configuration method, i.e. establishing a connection in the new network before the actual handoff takes place.

- **Average Jitter By Varying The Speed Of MN**

After plotting the graph for average jitter, we observed that the jitter remains almost constant for these three approaches with little variation in MIP. We also observed it is lesser in FHMIP and then HMIP and then MIP. The graph for jitter is shown in the figure-6.4 below:

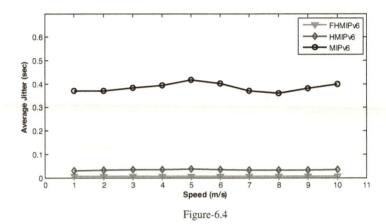

Figure-6.4

We again took some results for the same performance metrics by increasing the simulation time from 80 seconds to 160 seconds.

6.2   Results Obtained By Increasing the Simulation Time

The first result in this case obtained is taken at simulation time 80 seconds and at MN speed of 1m/s, so the first table in this case will also be similar to Table-6.1. Then we took results at simulation time 90 seconds to 160 seconds. The results in the tabular form are shown on the next page.

Performance Metrics	FHMIPv6	HMIPv6	MIPv6
Gen. or sent packets	13568	12460	12468
Received Pkts.	13108	9644	7769
Pkt. delivery Ratio (%)	96.6097	77.3996	62.3115
Dropped pkts	84	102	106
Avg. end-to-end delay (ms)	8.7598	8.73209	8.7321
Control packets	13451	12338	12367
Avg. routing load	44.8367	41.1267	41.2233
Avg. throughput (kbps)	615.23	564.06	563.61
Avg. handover-delay (secs)	0.22552	2.17132	3.26544
Avg. jitter (secs)	0.00562	0.03248	0.37142

Table 6.11- simulation time 90 secs

Performance metrics	FHMIPv6	HMIPv6	MIPv6
Gen. or sent packets	15243	14145	14154
Received Pkts.	14768	10949	8833
Pkt. delivery Ratio (%)	96.6214	77.4054	62.4063
Dropped pkts	80	92	96
Avg end-to-end delay (ms)	8.76	8.73257	8.73258
Control packets	15107	14014	14039
Avg. routing load	50.3567	46.7133	46.7967
Avg. throughput (kbps)	619.05	573.41	569.25
Avg. handover-delay (secs)	1.31775	2.38745	3.11875
Avg. jitter (secs)	0.00554	0.03374	0.38471

Table 6.12- simulation time 100 secs

Performance Metrics	FHMIPv6	HMIPv6	MIPv6
Gen. or sent packets	16926	15829	15831
Received Pkts.	16362	12266	9901
Pkt. delivery Ratio (%)	96.6678	77.4906	62.5418
Dropped pkts	90	92	97
Avg end-to-end delay (ms)	8.76011	8.73295	8.73295
Control packets	16781	15692	15695
Avg. routing load	55.9367	52.3067	52.3167
Avg.throughput (kbps)	622.20	581.02	577.63
Avg. handover-delay (secs)	1.30927	2.37554	3.11875
Avg. jitter (secs)	0.00577	0.03469	0.39451

Table 6.13- simulation time 110 secs

Performance metrics	FHMIPv6	HMIPv6	MIPv6
Gen. or sent packets	18608	17513	17520
Received Pkts.	17998	13577	10971
Pkt. delivery Ratio (%)	96.7218	77.5252	62.6198
Dropped pkts	90	92	96
Avg end-to-end delay (ms)	8.7602	8.73325	8.73326
Control packets	18453	17360	17385
Avg. routing load	61.51	57.8667	57.95
Avg.throughput (kbps)	625.05	587.25	582.47
Avg. handover-delay (secs)	1.89625	2.46546	3.24442
Avg. jitter (secs)	0.00595	0.03621	0.41792

Table 6.14- simulation time 120 secs

Performance metrics	FHMIPv6	HMIPv6	MIPv6
Gen. or sent packets	20286	19199	19204
Received Pkts.	19624	14886	12026
Pkt. delivery Ratio (%)	96.7367	77.5352	62.6223
Dropped pkts	96	102	106
Avg end-to-end delay (ms)	8.76027	8.7335	8.7335
Control packets	20119	19036	19055
Avg. routing load	67.0633	63.4533	63.5167
Avg.throughput (kbps)	627.12	592.66	587.22
Avg. handover-delay (Secs)	2.01175	2.77228	3.27479
Avg. jitter (secs)	0.00576	0.03589	0.40265

Table 6.15- simulation time 130 secs

Performance metrics	FHMIPv6	HMIPv6	MIPv
Gen. or sent packets	21974	20877	2089
Received Pkts.	21262	16192	1308
Pkt. delivery Ratio (%)	96.7598	77.5590	62.64
Dropped pkts	96	102	106
Avg. end-to-end delay (ms)	8.76034	8.73371	8.733
Control packets	21797	20704	2073
Avg. routing load	72.6567	69.0133	69.12
Avg. throughput(kbps)	629.07	597.16	592.
Avg. handover-delay (secs)	2.54317	2.89503	3.364
Avg. jitter (secs)	0.00569	0.03321	0.371

Table 6.16-simulation time 140 secs

Performance Metrics	FHMIPv6	HMIPv6	MIPv6
Gen. or sent packets	23651	22561	22569
Received Pkts.	22880	17489	14131
Pkt. delivery Ratio (%)	96.7401	77.5187	62.6124
Dropped pkts	96	102	106
Avg. end-to-end delay (ms)	8.76039	8.73389	8.73389
Control packets	23455	22374	22395
Avg. routing load	78.1833	74.58	74.65
Avg. throughput (kbps)	630.69	601.03	596.25
Avg. handover-delay (secs)	2.89513	2.98445	3.42582
Avg. jitter (secs)	0.00552	0.03299	0.36161

Table 6.17- simulation time 150 secs

Performance metrics	FHMIPv6	HMIPv6	MIPv
Gen. or sent packets	25340	24238	2382
Received Pkts.	24524	18796	1492
Pkt. delivery Ratio (%)	96.7798	77.5476	62.62
Dropped pkts	106	113	116
Avg. end-to-end delay (ms)	8.76043	8.73404	8.73
Control packets	25135	24018	2361
Avg. routing load	83.7833	80.66	78.71
Avg. throughput (kbps)	632.05	604.19	598.4
Avg. handover-delay (secs)	2.90425	3.08722	3.561
Avg. jitter (secs)	0.00564	0.03317	0.381

Table 6.18- simulation time 160 secs

After obtaining the results by increasing the simulation time from 80 seconds to 160 seconds, we plotted the graphs for the performance metrics (PDF, Avg. handover delay, Avg. throughput and Avg. jitter).

- **Packet Delivery Ratio By Increasing Simulation Time**

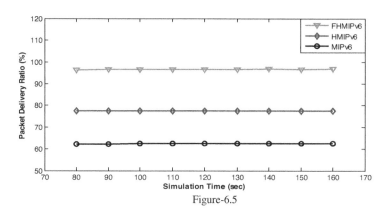

Figure-6.5

- **Average Handover Delay By Increasing The Simulation Time**

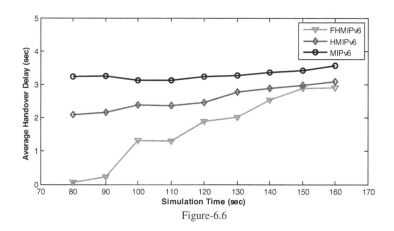

Figure-6.6

From the figure-6.5 and figure-6.6, it is observed that the lines follow the same trend as we saw in the previous scenario by varying the speed of MN. In case of packet delivery ratio it follows the trend FHMIP>HMIP>MIP and in case of average handoff delay is follows the reverse trend.

- **Average Throughput By Increasing The Simulation Time**

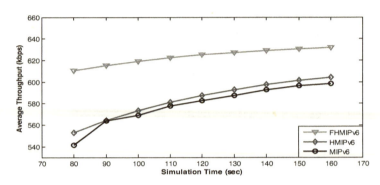

Figure-6.7

Figure-6.7 shows the comparison among the three mobile IP approaches for average throughput by increasing the simulation time. It is again following the same trend as FHMIP>HMIP>MIP with little variation that the throughput is increasing with increase in simulation time. The reason behind this is that more number of packets are delivered by increasing the simulation time and thus more data is transferred per unit time in kbps. Maximum TP obtained for FHMIP is 632kbps, for HMIP is 604kbps and for MIP is 598kbps.

- **Average Jitter By Increasing The Simulation Time**

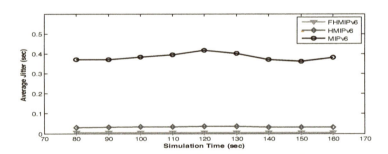

Figure-6.8

42

As we see from the figure-6.8, jitter follows the same trend as in the previous case. And there are no variations seen in average jitter by increasing the simulation time.

6.3 Result Analysis

In our simulation of mobile IP approaches for handover delay and network performance as well, we have focused on the comparison of standard mobile IP, HMIP and FHMIP for handover delay, packet delivery ratio, throughput and jitter. The total delay involves the layer two (L2) delay, the address resolution time and layer three (L3) handover delay.

The TCP session between the CN and the MN starts after 5 seconds of the simulation, the packet size was 1000 bytes. We run the simulation first for varying speed of MN and second by increasing the simulation time.

From the simulation results we got the measured handover delay for FHMIP is minimum at walking speed (1m/s) i.e. 55.44 ms which is much lesser than that in case of HMIP which has 2171ms handover delay and MIP which has 3118ms of handover delay. Also we measured the average throughput and packet delivery ratio and we got maximum throughput and PDF in FHMIP and then in HMIP and then MIP.

The simulation results clearly show that the FHMIP approach has better performance in terms of handover delay, packets loss, PDF and average throughput as compared to the standard mobile IP protocol and HMIP.

FHMIP protocol can help efficiently to reduce the total handover delay and the total packets loss which generated from the handover process, but it still needs more efforts to reduce the signaling overhead and to reduce the delay to a value that can meet the real time applications requirements for a seamless handover.

The mathematical calculations in the chapter 4 have also shown that FHMIP has the minimum handover delay compared to the standard mobile IP and HMIP.

The simulation results also show that the handover delay is still far from the theoretical calculation as we increase the speed of MN or when we increase the simulation time, and still not sufficient to satisfy the real time applications requirements to support the seamless roaming. Much more effort must be done to reduce the delay further more.

CHAPTER 7: CONCLUSION AND FUTURE WORK

7.1 Conclusion

The study of many handover delay reduction approaches has been shown by this thesis work. The new suggested FHMIPv6 considered specifically, and compared to the standard mobile IP protocol and HMIPv6.

The simulation results show that the FHMIP has better performance in terms of total handover delay, packet loss, packet delivery ratio and throughput as well, compared to the standard mobile IP protocol and HMIP.

The simulation results also show that a minimum handover delay is achieved in FHMIP, which is still not sufficient to satisfy the real time application requirements for a smooth handover process in order to keep an ongoing session without any disruption.

7.2 Future Work

The work in this thesis was focused in the linear movement for the mobile node. We suggest that the future work will be focused more on the random movement and stationary movement for the mobile node.

These protocols can be used in conjunction with latest technologies like Source Specific Multicast (SSM) and can be studied for mobile internet related applications involving audio, video streaming and other real time communications. Both mobility and SSM find their application in upcoming fields like e-learning, IP-television etc.

References:

[1] J.Kempf, Ed., "Problem Statement for Network-Based Localizedb Mobility Management (NETLMM)," IETF Request for Comments 4830, April 2007.

[2] Jun Lei; Xiaoming Fu; , "Evaluating the Benefits of Introducing PMIPv6 for Localized Mobility Management," Wireless Communications and Mobile Computing Conference, 2008. IWCMC '08. International , vol., no., pp.74-80, 6-8 Aug. 2008.

[3] J.Kempf, Ed., "Goals for Network-Based Localized Mobility Management (NETLMM)," IETF Request for Comments 4831, April 2007.

[4] C. Perkins, "IP Mobility Support for IPv4", RFC 3344, Aug.2002.

[5] D. Johnson, C. E. Perkins, and J. Arkko, "Mobility Support in IPv6," IETF Request for Comments 3775, June 2004.

[6] T. et al. Neighbor Discovery for IP Version 6. RFC 2461, December 1998.

[7] Hesham Soliman, "Hierarchical MIPv6 mobility management (HMIPv6)" IETF Mobile IP Working Group, july 2001.

[8] Wang Lixin, Jian Yingxia, Zheng Dawer and Chen Zhixin, "HMIPv6-based Handover Optimized Solution and Performance Analysis" IETF, IEEE 2010.

[9] Myung-Kyu Yi, Jin-Woo Choi, and Young-Kyu Yang, "A Comparative Analysis on the Signaling Load of Proxy Mobile IPv6 and Hierarchical Mobile IPv6" IEEE 2009.

[10] Xavier P´erez-Costa, Marc Torrent-Moreno, Hannes Hartenstein, "A Performance Comparison of Mobile IPv6, Hierarchical Mobile IPv6, Fast Handovers for Mobile IPv6 and their Combination" Mobile Computing and Communications Review, Volume 7, Number 4.

[11] G. Dommety et al., "Fast Handovers for Mobile IPv6", Internet Draft, IETF, March 2002. Work in Progress.

[12] Ivov, E.; Montavont, J.; Noel, T.; , "Thorough empirical analysis of the IETF FMIPv6 protocol over IEEE 802.11 networks," *Wireless Communications, IEEE* , vol.15, no.2, pp.65-72, April 2008.

[13] Aaron Balchunas, "IPv4 Addressing and Subnetting" IPv4 Addressing and Subnetting v1.33, 2012.

[14] J. Gnana Jayanthi, S. Albert Rabara, "IPv6 Addressing Architecture in IPv4 Network" Second International Conference on Communication Software and Networks, 2010.

[15] Kang-won Lee; Won-Kyeong Seo; Dong-Won Kum; You-Ze Cho; , "Global Mobility Management Scheme with Interworking between PMIPv6 and MIPv6," Networking and Communications, 2008. WIMOB '08. IEEE International Conference on Wireless and Mobile Computing, vol., no., pp.153-158, 12-14 Oct. 2008.

[16] F. Belghoul, Y. Moret, C. Bonnet, "Performance comparison and analysis on MIPv6, fast MIPv6 bi-casting and Eurecom IPv6 soft handover over IEEE 802.11b WLANs", 2004 IEEE 59th VTC, 2004- Spring. Vol. 5, 17-19 May 2004, pp.2672 – 2676.

[17] J. Lai, Y. Ahmet Sekercioglu, N. Jordan, A. Pitsillides, "Performance Evaluation of Mobile IPv6 Handover Extensions in an IEEE 802.11b Wireless Network Environment", Proceedings of ISCC '06, 26-29 Jun. 2006, pp.161- 166.

[18] J. Tian, and S. Helal, "Performance of MIP/WLAN in Rapid Mobility Environments", University of Florida, Gainesville, FL 32611-6120, USA, IEEE Explorer, 2006.

[19] L. Dimopoulou, G. Leoleis, I.O. Venieris, "Fast handover support in a WLAN environment: challenges and perspectives", IEEE Network, Vol. 19, Issue 3, May-Jun. 2005 pp.14 - 20.

[20] Zongpu Jia, Gaolei Wang and Ran Zhao, "A Literature Survey on Handoff for Mobile IPv6" Journal Of Networks, Vol. 6, No. 8, August 2011.

[21] Jia Zongpu, Wang Hongmei, Xue Xiao, Jia Ziyu, "Analysis and Optimization for Handover Performance of Mobile IPv6 Based Ping-Pong Mode" IEEE 2008.

[22] Xavier Pérez Costa, Ralf Schmitz, Hannes Hartenstein, Marco Liebsch, "A MIPv6, FMIPv6 and HMIPv6 handover latency study: analytical approach" IETF, IEEE 2003.

[23] Petri Jokela, Teemu Rinta-aho, Tony Jokikyyny, Jorma Wall, Martti Kuparinen, Heikki Mahkonen, Jan Melén, Tero Kauppinen, Jouni Korhonen, "Handover Performance with HIP and MIPv6" IEEE 2005.

[24] Chao Fan, lun Liu, Wei Guo, "Implement Scheme of MIPv6 and Improvement of hand over delay based on Adhoc network on Linux" 3rd International Conference on Advanced Computer Theory and Engineering (ICACTE) 2010.

[25] Xinyi WU, Gang NIE, "Comparison of Different Mobility Management Schemes for Reducing handover Latency in Mobile IPv6" International Conference on Industrial Mechatronics and Automation, 2009.

[26] Hong-Sun Jun and Miae Woo, "Performance Analysis of Multicast-based Localized Mobility Support Scheme in IPv6 Networks" Proceedings of the Second Annual Conference on Communication Networks and Services Research (CNSR'04), IEEE 2004.

[27] Rajeev Koodli, "IP Address Location Privacy and Mobile IPv6" draft-ietf-mip6-location-privacy-ps-05.txt, IETF 2 february 2007.

[28] Shaima Qureshi, M. Ahsan Chishti and Ajaz H. Mir, "Mobility Management in Next Generation Networks (Analysis of Handover in Host and Network Based Mobility Protocols)" ICCIT 2012.

[29] Huei-Wen Ferng, Wen-Yan Kao, Jeng-Ji Huang and David Shiung, "A Dynamic Resource Reservation Scheme Designed for Improving Multicast Protocols in HMIPv6-Based Networks" IEEE 2006.

[30] Jianfeng Guan, Yajuan Qin, Shuai Gao, Hongke Zhang, "The Performance Analysis Of Multicast In Proxy Mobile Ipv6" Proceedings of ICCTA2009, IEEE 2009.

[31] Sangjin Jeong, Myung-Ki Shin and Hyoug-Jun Kim, "A Handover Scheme Supporting IPv4 IPv6 Traversal over Network-based Mobility Management Domains" Feb. 12-14, 2007 ICACT2007.

[32] Ki-Sik Kong and Wonjun Lee, Youn-Hee Han, Myung-Ki Shin, "Handover Latency Analysis of a Network-Based Localized Mobility Management Protocol" ICC 2008.

[33] Long Le and Marco Liebsch, "Preliminary Binding: An Extension to Proxy Mobile IPv6 for Inter-Technology Handover" WCNC 2009 proceedings.

[34] Hsieh, R., and Seneviratne, "A Comparison of Mechanisms for Improving Mobile IP Handoff Latency for End-to-End TCP", *MobiCom'03*, San Diego, California, USA, September 14-19, 2003.

[35] "The Network Simulator – *ns* (version 2) Website", http://www.isi.edu/nsnam.

[36] "The NS Manual", http://www.isi.edu/nsnam/ns/ns-documentation.html

YOUR KNOWLEDGE HAS VALUE

- We will publish your bachelor's and master's thesis, essays and papers

- Your own eBook and book - sold worldwide in all relevant shops

- Earn money with each sale

Upload your text at www.GRIN.com
and publish for free

www.ingramcontent.com/pod-product-compliance
Lightning Source LLC
La Vergne TN
LVHW092353060326
832902LV00008B/1002